How To Approach Standards Chromatically

Techniques of Superimposition
by
David Liebman

Transcriptions and Music Engraving by Matt Vashlishan
Cover Design by Benjamin Gritton

Published by
JAMEY AEBERSOLD JAZZ®
P.O. Box 1244
New Albany, IN 47151-1244
www.jazzbooks.com
ISBN 978-1-56224-029-5

Table of Contents

Eb PART TRANSCRIPTIONS OF DAVID'S SOLOS . . . . Page   Track #

Notes from David Liebman

I have covered the objective of this project in the spoken introduction at the beginning of the CD itself. Following is a summary and recapitulation of the main points, along with a tune by tune description of the superimposition techniques used on each track.

The very notion of superimposition is closely related to common practice reharmonization techniques, whereby musicians invent a new chord progression to accompany a given melody (usually a standard song). In the case of superimposition relevant to my chromatic approach used here, I did not have the usual challenge of matching melody notes to a specific reharmonized chord progression. The main concern here was how to incorporate new melodic material for improvising that by and large does not reference the proscribed chords or modes, but instead is based on contrasting "chromatic" colors. For theses purposes superimposition is a means to an end; a way to discover and organize other tones which may be "foreign" to the given chord(s). The overriding premise is the creation of new and interesting melodies, just as in normal diatonic improvisation.

In a real playing situation, it is highly improbable that any one method of superimposition would exist by itself for the duration of an entire improvisation as on this recording. It is the constant mixture of several ways of thinking and hearing which is above all appropriate to the material as well as respecting the specific idiom and musicians performing. The closest examples in this volume of mixing together several superimposition methods are my solos on the blues and rhythm changes formats, where I didn't follow a set sequence as elsewhere. Also, any one method used on a specific song does not mean it is only applicable for that progression; the superimposition techniques are theoretically interchangeable. Again, the only limitation is taste and appropriateness.

Examples 1-7 ("Girl From Ipanema" through "Rhythm Changes") are concerned with some of the more common standard chord progressions, while examples 8-11 involve modal and pedal point frameworks. (Example 12, "Off A Bird" is based on interval sets or the "time, no changes" idiom which exists as its own category). The kind of chromaticism I use throughout this volume is applicable to any normal diatonic harmonic situation, be it simple II-V progressions as in "Satin Doll" or modulating keys as in "Donna Lee." Overall my chromatic approach sounds most natural in the idioms of modal and pedal type tunes because of the more obvious openness of the underlying harmony. But one must address the issue of common chord progressions, which I attempted to do in this volume.

I noted in my spoken introduction an important point concerning phrasing that should be kept in mind while listening to the solos. I have purposely de-emphasized personal stylistic traits such as the use of different and varied rhythms, expressive nuances (trills, grace notes, vibrato, etc.) and other miscellaneous factors that would and should be present in any good jazz solo. I did this (not easily I must say) so that the listener would not confuse "how" something is played with "what" is played. In the final analysis, as in any music, what counts most is feeling and expression. But for the pedagogical purposes of this volume I tried to minimize these and other "expressive" aspects.

In the final result, dissonance and consonance are relative terms, differing not only for entire musical eras (such as the Classical period of Mozart compared to the late Romantics, etc), but also on a personal level. What is dissonant to one individual will necessarily sound different to another. This is the beauty of art-it is as the cliché states in the eyes (or in this case, the ears) of the beholder. One could never state unilaterally that such and such a sound heard by another set of ears can be categorized as dissonant, consonant, etc. Of course we make generalizations and assume there is a common aesthetic, but in reality that is not true. Everything is personal when it comes to taste. My hope is that interested musicians will be open to change and personal growth regardless of whether the material here is new or intimidating. What appears to sound strange and foreign today may be commonplace tomorrow. I know that when I first started listening to my main influence, John Coltrane, in the early 1960's it was very difficult. But with time, it became familiar and inspiring.

You are being provided with several solos transcribed by Matt Vashlishan. Please refer to my DVD on this subject ("The Improviser's Guide to Transcription"-Caris Music Service) which explains in great detail my method of how to get the most from a transcription. In the case of the solos transcribed here, one need not necessarily play along note by note, but rather attempt to analyze the kinds of lines I am playing on the superimposed progressions and check out where I use chord and non chord tones, arpeggio type ideas and so on. Then attempt to improvise in a similar vein using the transcriptions and superimposed progressions as a model. Chordalists may turn the accompanying piano off and try to find appropriate voicings (which are discussed in detail in my "Chromatic Approach to Jazz Melody and Harmony" published by Advance Music). For the sake of convenience the original play along tracks are included. I urge you to explore one tune at a time and attempt to get a feel of whichever method pertains to that example. The essential learning attitude should be that this is a process towards conceiving, hearing and feeling lines of any nature on any given material; to not be locked into only one or two ways of conceiving of lines.

Have a great time; I hope this leads to an expansion of your ear, mind and heart!!

Stroudsburg, PA USA

Spring 2006

My sincere thanks to:

Matt Vashlishan, for transcription and copying work beyond the call of duty.

Steve Good, for his impeccable engineering.

Jamey, for taking a chance!!

The Material

The sequence of the songs is purposeful as I progress up the "dissonant food-chain." In other words, the first example on "Girl From Ipanema" is based on upper structures of the proscribed chords, resulting in a simple and relatively consonant method of superimposition, whereas by the time one progresses to "A Love Supreme" the harmonic/melodic clashes are much more intense.

One final note about playing in a real situation, vis a vis chromatic notes against whatever chords are being played. A comper (chord accompanist) need not have perfect pitch (wouldn't hurt of course) but should have enough experience in playing this way in order to hear the change of color and voice their chords in such a way as to be in synch with the chromatic notes. It is not an ear training exercise; musicality and the desire to create a meaningful statement rule above all.

The general format I followed on each tune was that the first chorus is meant to be a simpler "melodic" improvisation evolving to using the proscribed superimpositions more literally. The last chorus(es) designated as "combinations" is when I play in a looser manner, as well as using a bit more rhythmic complexity.

A few definitions to be clear about:

"Chord" or "scale quality" means any of the five families: major, minor, diminished, augmented and dominant.

"Proscribed" roots or home key means the roots and/or key that are written in the original tune.

1. GIRL FROM IPANEMA: upper structure chords   As a standard tune with one of the cleverest combinations of harmony and melody written (Jobim wrote a lot of small masterpieces), I used it to emphasize a basic principle of superimposition, which is to emphasize the upper structure of any given chord in melodic constructs. For example, looking at the first chord, Fmaj7 (referring to concert pitch throughout these notes) and reconfigure it as G triad/F major 7th (which translates to an Fmaj13#11), you would melodically emphasize the upper G triad. Since this "superimposition" is really nothing more than extending the given diatonic chord, the overall sound of upper structure playing is not much different than normal, but does give the melodicist a different vantage point for creating lyrical and possibly more arpeggiated type lines. I have notated the upper structures that I am playing. In this case, there will be no real harmonic "clashing" with the harmonicist's chords. Due to space considerations, this tune is written out a bit differently than all the others. The first chorus indicates the regular chord changes with the ensuing ones showing the chord progression I was using.

2. DONNA LEE: tritone relationship   The tri-tone relationship is well documented in jazz harmony texts and has been part of the improviser's language certainly since Charlie Parker's era if not on occasion before. The concept here is similar to the upper structure methodology demonstrated above, meaning that a tritone substitute is made up of the altered tones of the original chord (at least in the case of dominant chords). If the improviser orients his lines to the tritone substitute, there is a subtle color change from the original progression which emphasizes the inherent tension. Though there may be a bit of a clash with the comping instrument, it is fleetingly perceived.

3. AUTUMN LEAVES: II -V substitutes   This tune represents one of the most basic harmonic frameworks in the standard repertoire moving between major and relative minor home keys. The superimposition principle at work is that any II-V progression can be substituted for the original and still portray the feeling of subdominant-dominant-movement (which is after all what II-V implies). The crucial factor in this method is to play a very clear and "inside" line on the resolving I chord which in most cases remains intact from the original progression. The principle is that II-V movement, no matter the relationship of the final I chord to the progression, will portray a resolving tendency. Of course, with trial and error a good improviser will eventually be able to cognize exactly which of the possible superimposed II-V progressions work in a particular situation (theoretically meaning any other of the eleven key choices); all to be determined by the tension/release aspects desired. The idea of relative dissonance being strategically placed in a solo is beyond the scope of this volume, but essentially it is no different than choosing between one or another form of a dominant chord:G7 b9 b13 versus G7 +9 +11 for example as a choice for usage. In general II-V movement that has more common tones in agreement with the proscribed/ original progression will be perceived as less dissonant than one that has more foreign tones.

4. TAKE THE 'A' TRAIN: Giant Steps movement   Using this simple and classic Duke Ellington harmonic progression which features relatively long durations of chords, the method used here is an extension of the classic John Coltrane substitute cycle made famous not only in that tune itself, "Giant Steps," but also as demonstrated on standards like "But Not For Me," "Body and Soul," "The Night Has 1000 Eyes" and others. Though for the most part Trane stayed on the original progression of ascending half step, descending fifth, ascending minor third, etc. (over an existing II-V progression), I have extended this movement to imply upward and downward motion, mostly but not exclusively in thirds and fifths with an avoidance of symmetrical patterns whenever possible. One of the guidelines is that any V chord can resolve to a I chord, even if it is transitory and not necessarily related to one of the existing proscribed harmonic centers of the original progression. Furthermore, the relative II chord attached to each new dominant can be slipped in as well. Chord quality (major, minor, etc) is not as important as is the feeling of root movement. The line player doesn't have to do much more than arpeggiate the substitutes to achieve the desired effect of movement. The clash between the proscribed harmony and the substitutes will be very evident here.

5. SATIN DOLL: side slipping   This term was popularized by the great educator/saxophonist Jerry Coker in his classic book on improvisation and the jazz language ("Improvising Jazz"). Basically, it means playing a half step above or below the proscribed chord resulting in the most dissonant of all harmonic-melodic clashes. With constant reference back and forth to the proscribed root and chord, the illusion of fleeting dissonance can be effective. Remember that no one substitute method exists by itself in a real playing situation, but would be mixed and matched with the other concepts presented in this volume.

6/7. RHYTHM and BLUES CHANGES: combining all of above methods   I used the old war horses of blues and rhythm changes in the most common keys to freely combine all of the concepts above and improvise in a more natural manner for a few choruses. For the purpose of this CD, these two examples are the closest to a real playing situation, albeit without the conversational aspect and interplay between myself and a rhythm section described in detail above.

8. IMPRESSIONS: moving chord cycles   Using this most celebrated modal progression (originating as its source in Miles Davis' "So What"), this method implies the use of superimposed chord progressions against the stationary modal backdrop. The goal is to outline a set of changes as if they were being literally played, but with a conscious effort to avoid any symmetrical or familiar sounding patterns in the movement (cycle of fifths, Giant Steps, tri tones, side slipping, etc). Quartal voicings in the mode which most commonly accompanies this modal style are appropriate since their intervallic combinations tend to obscure the primacy of one root over another. As mentioned in the intro notes, from the aesthetic standpoint, the idea is to be able to organize other pitches away from the given mode in a manner that is musical and sonically organized. To be avoided are endless streams of eighth or sixteenth notes outlining an unending cascade of superimposed changes; as well one should incorporate varied harmonic rhythms rather than having every chord always lasting for two beats as I have done here for the sake of comprehension. It is the juxtaposition of the pitches emanating from the superimposed progression in conjunction WITH and AGAINST the original proscribed framework that is the overriding goal. Note that these "random" progressions used here do have the home key played at some point in each eight bar phrase. This home key can be placed at a variety of junctures loosely near the beginning or end of an eight or sixteen bar phrase.

9. INDIA: stationary pedal point using scale/chord quality superimposition   This tune references a pedal point concept (G), rather than the above "Impressions" moving modes format. The method here employs the well established device of using the proscribed root but changing the chord/scale quality to create a variety of different scale colors above the stationary pedal. Bill Evans used this method a lot in his diatonic language, for example changing a minor 7th chord to a dominant #9 chords (D-7th became D7#9). In fact on this version played by my working group (Vol.81) pianist Phil Markowitz instinctively used this technique on the original play along version, even without me soloing at the time. Again, as in "Impressions," one could be pretty confident that a sympathetic accompanist would hear the color change and comp accordingly. Relatively speaking, this superimposition method is very subtle and less dissonant than some of the previous concepts or ones to follow. I have indicated the modes in the order I played them with the timings of when they enter the improvisation.

10. LOFT DANCE: using other roots of home key mode for parallel and/or opposing scale/chord substitution
Of all the methods used here, this one is probably the most difficult to realize against a pre-existing played progression (the original play along track). I am using any of the pitches from the proscribed scale (accompanying each chord) as a potential root for another chord/scale. For example, the first chord here is Gbmaj7#4. The available notes for finding a substitute color are any of the pitches of the Gb lydian (Ab,Bb,C,Db,Eb,F) with the same rational for the next three chords of the tune. For the first two example types (choruses 4 through 9) I stayed with the same chord quality as the original, therefore only the root is different. For the next two choruses, I changed not only the root, but as well the chord quality, thereby heightening the tension a bit more. Throughout the solo, I try to alternate substitution and original.

11. A LOVE SUPREME: using non-home key notes as roots   This extends the concept used above in "Loft Dance," in this case using pitches other than those from the home key. In this example those possible roots would be everything NOT in the proscribed home key of F dorian (meaning Gb,A,B,Db,E), once again in parallel or contrasting chord qualities. My playing on this track is by necessity a bit more stylistically idiosyncratic than the others because the underlying rhythmic feeling suggests melodic lines other than the customary eighth note type. The timings of when I changed modalities is indicated.

12. OFF A BIRD: intervallic   Intervallic thinking could be said to permeate all playing, regardless of harmonic or non-harmonic implications. In other words, as soon as you put two notes together, you are in essence playing intervallically. This example stands apart from all the others in the project in that there is no harmonic thinking, only intervallic as the basis for my improvisation. We refer to this idiom as "time, no changes" (also called "free-bop"). It means that though there exists the usual familiar walking time rhythmic foundation, there is no given tonal center. (Of course in real time, tonal centers may arise as a result of several possible scenarios: a repetitive pedal tone or ostinato figure, converging counterpoint lines between two or more instruments or even a clearly outlined diatonic melody.)

My "Chromatic Approach to Jazz Melody and Harmony" book spends some time on this as a separate topic, but I wanted to include it here for completeness. I have divided the organization of intervals into three categories: major and minor 2nds, major and minor 3rds and 6ths; perfect and augmented 4ths with perfect 5ths; major and minor 7ths and 9ths. You should be able to discern when I am switching interval sets. The idea for this example is to concentrate on one set, "milking" those intervals. Of course in a real playing situation, all the intervals would be mixed together. Having control of interval sets in an organized fashion is a worthwhile goal for improvising in any style.

Notes About the Transcriptions and the Transcribing Process
by Matt Vashlishan

Transcribing is probably one of the most important things one can do to learn about improvisation and improve their playing. Needless to say, when I was asked to take on this project I was very excited to get way more in depth to the techniques that Dave Liebman covers in his "Chromatic Approach to Jazz Harmony and Melody". At sea for four months playing a gig aboard a cruise ship, I decided that I had more than enough time to get into this the old fashioned way. I put everything onto a tape recorder (to be able to rewind/fast forward easier than a CD player) and transcribed it without slowing anything down. For my playing at a fairly young twenty three years old, it proved to be one of the best projects I have ever done. Transcribing it was one thing, and then becoming absorbed in it over and over again during the countless hours of transferring the music to the computer really helped me understand what Lieb was doing on each of these tracks.

Lucky for me, Dave slightly simplified his playing for this volume, emphasizing the pitches themselves, limiting his usually expansive expressive style. As he still uses a few techniques (glissandos, bending notes, vibrato, various articulations and alternate fingerings to name a few), I chose not to notate them to keep things simple and easier to read. The most difficult of Lieb's expressive devices is to notate his use of time, when he plays ahead or behind the beat. In some transcriptions this is usually indicated by an arrow pointing either backwards (behind) or forward (ahead). Again for the sake of clarity I decided not to use these symbols, instead choosing to write what I felt the general rhythm to be as if he was not changing the feel.

I have also made these solos easier to read and play for those not playing soprano or tenor saxophone. When David is playing tenor, the concert pitch solos are transposed up an octave to put everything in the staff therefore avoiding too many ledger lines as well as switching to and from bass clef. The Eb alto parts are mostly unison. I have transposed some notes up or down an octave in order to stay within the range between low Bb and high F#. I tried to avoid large or awkward leaps as best I could. However, I also found it great practice to learn the soprano solos on alto in unison throughout.

I had a great time putting these solos together and I hope you enjoy them.

David Liebman's solo to the superimposed chord changes of:

The Girl From Ipanema

(from Aebersold vol. 70)

4

Donna Lee
(from Aebersold vol. 6)

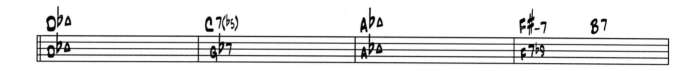

David Liebman's solo to the superimposed chord changes of:

Autumn Leaves
(from Aebersolo Vol. 54)

CD Track 7

6

8

9

10

Take The A-Train
(from Aebersold Vol. 12)

13

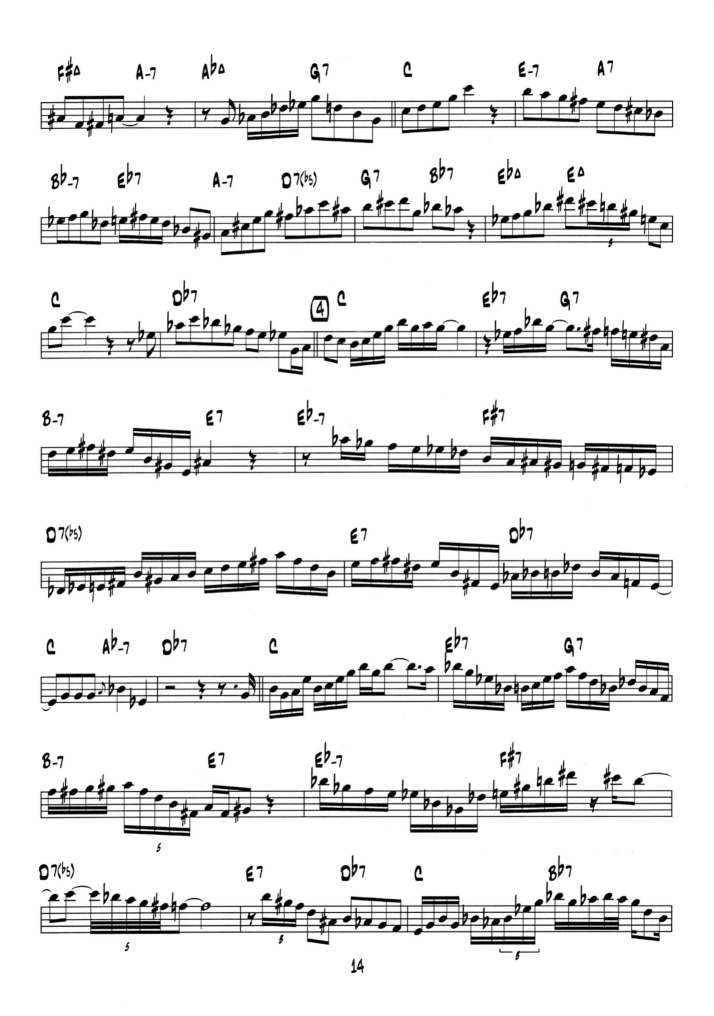

14

15

Satin Doll

(from Aebersolo vol. 12)

18

19

21

David Liebman's solo to the chord changes of:

F Blues

(from Aebersold Vol. 42)

23

24

David Liebman's solo to the chord changes of:

Rhythm Changes
(from Aebersold vol. 47)

26

27

28

IMPRESSIONS
(from Aebersolo vol. 28)

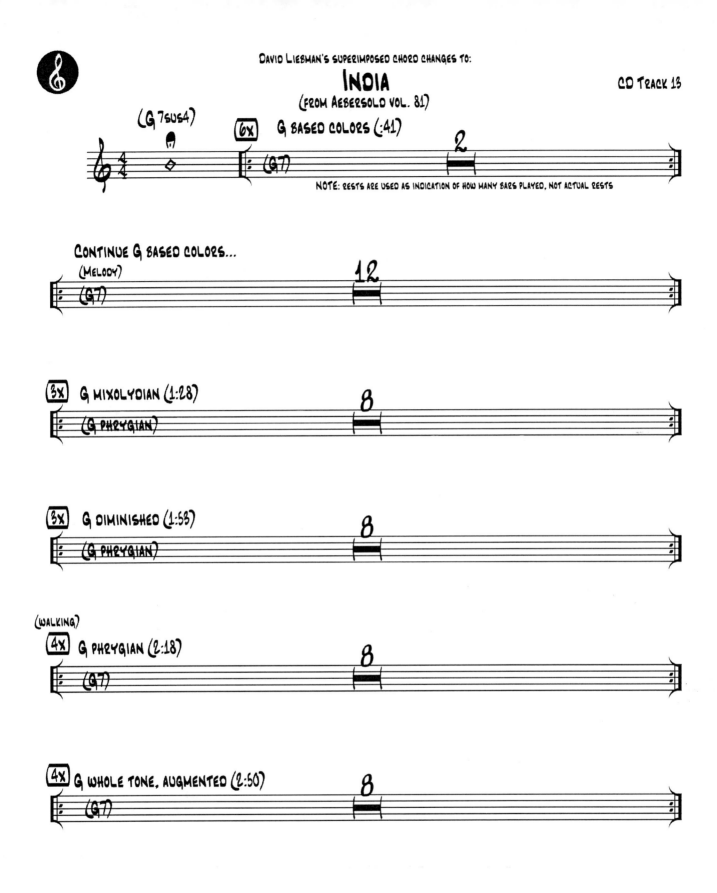

LOFT DANCE
(FROM AEBERSOLD VOL. 19)

LONG NOTES AROUND MELODY AND ORIGINAL PROGRESSION

NOTE: EACH CHORD IS PLAYED FOR 4 BARS THROUGHOUT!

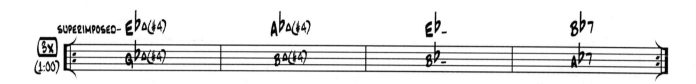

COMBINATIONS...

A Love Supreme
(from Aebersold vol. 28)

CD Track 15

APHRYGIAN (1:35)

BMAJOR (2:09)

Db MELODIC MINOR (2:42)

33

COMBINATIONS (3:15)

Major and Minor 2nds, 3rds, 6ths (0:40)

Maj. and Min. 7ths and 9ths (1:55)

36

COMBINATIONS (2:15)

37

David Liebman's solo to the superimposed chord changes of:

The Girl From Ipanema

(from Aebersolo vol. 70)

41

Donna Lee
(from Aebersolo vol. 6)

CD Track 6

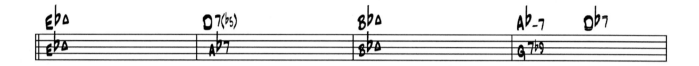

46

Take The A-Train

David Liebman's solo to the superimposed chord changes of:
(from Aebersold Vol. 12)

CD Track 8

50

51

54

SATIN DOLL

(FROM AEBERSOLD VOL. 12)

CD TRACK 9

57

58

59

DAVID LIEBMAN'S SOLO TO THE CHORD CHANGES OF:

F Blues
(FROM AEBERSOLD VOL. 42)

CD TRACK 10

Rhythm Changes
(from Aebersold vol. 47)

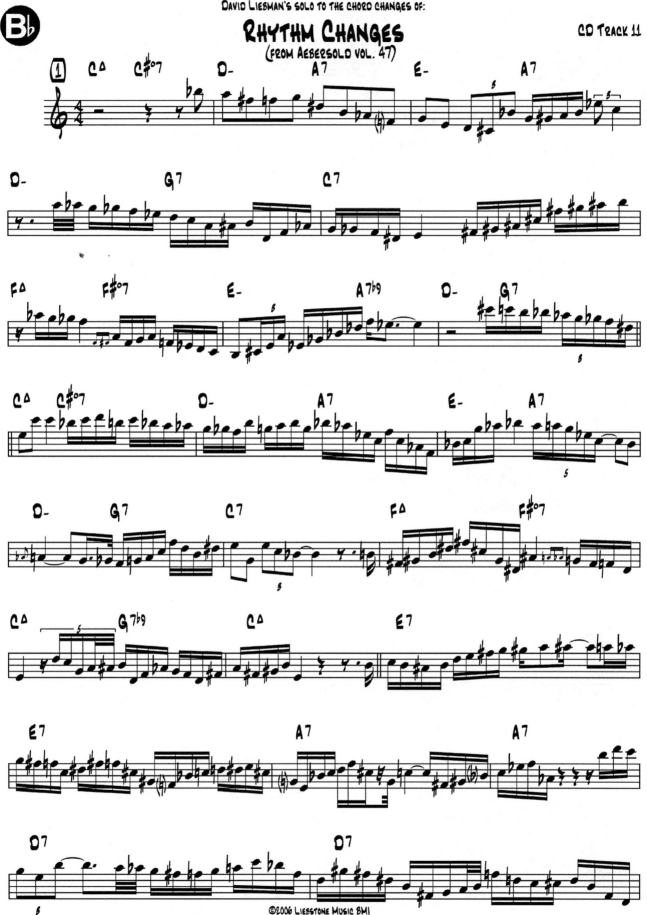

65

66

DAVID LIEBMAN'S SUPERIMPOSED CHORD CHANGES TO:

IMPRESSIONS

(FROM AEBERSOLD VOL. 28)

(EACH CHORUS PLAYED AABA)

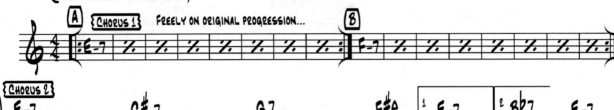

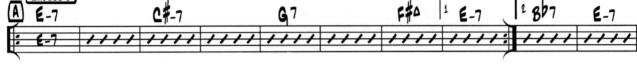

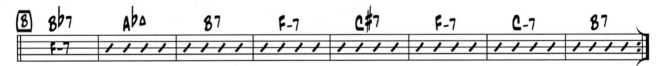

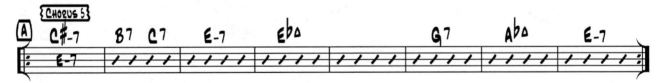

©2006 LIEBSTONE MUSIC BMI
INTERNATIONAL COPYRIGHT SECURED ALL RIGHTS RESERVED

67

David Liebman's superimposed chord changes to:

India

(from Aebersolo vol. 81)

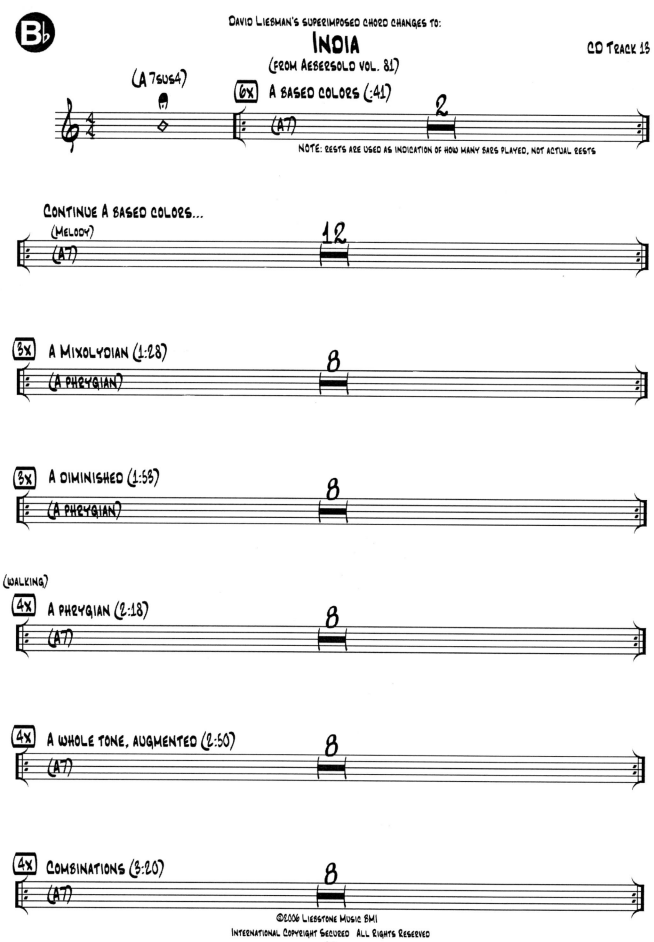

6X A based colors (:41)

NOTE: rests are used as indication of how many bars played, not actual rests

Continue A based colors...
(melody)

3X A Mixolydian (1:28)

3X A Diminished (1:53)

(walking)
4X A Phrygian (2:18)

4X A whole tone, augmented (2:50)

4X Combinations (3:20)

David Liebman's superimposed chord changes to:

LOFT DANCE
(from Aebersold vol. 19)

CD Track 14

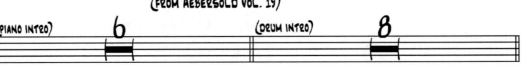

Bb

71

COMBINATIONS (3:15)

David Liebman's solo on:

Off A Bird
(from Aebersolo Vol. 81)

Bb

CD Track 16

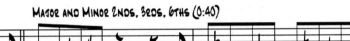

Major and Minor 2nds, 3rds, 6ths (0:40)

73

COMBINATIONS (2:15)

75

76

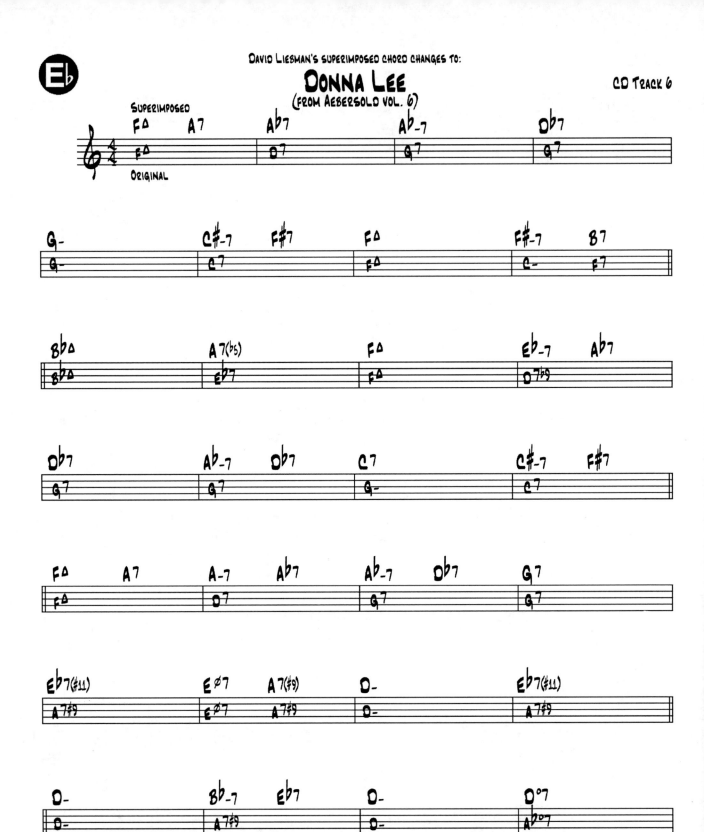

AUTUMN LEAVES
(from Aebersold Vol. 54)

CD Track 7

83

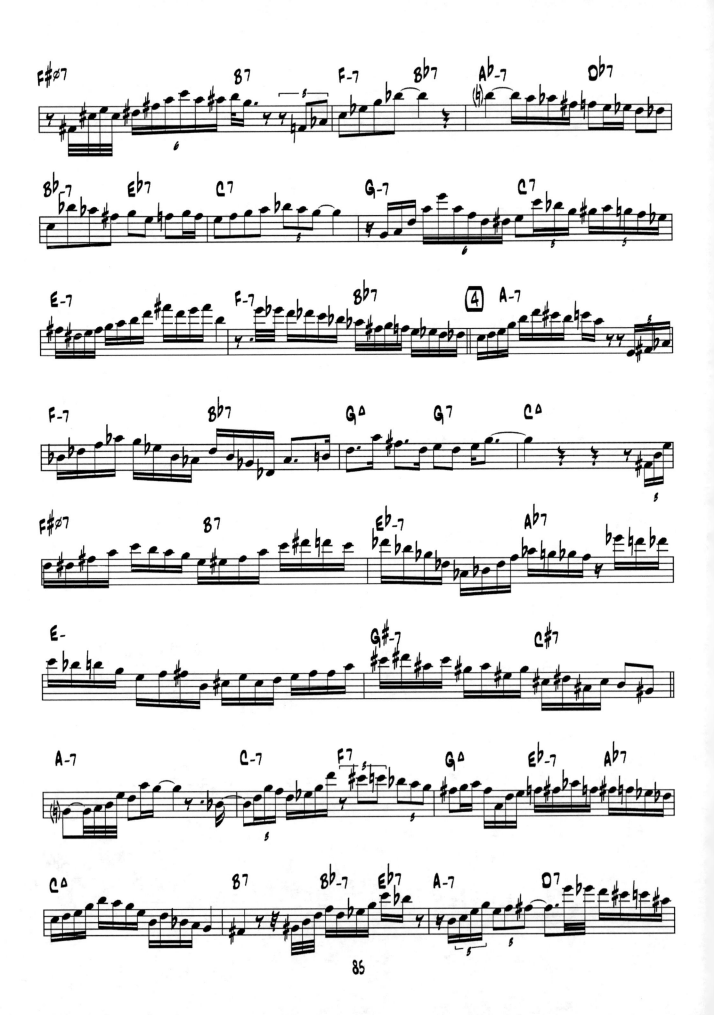

Take The A-Train
(from Aebersolo Vol. 12)

88

90

SATIN DOLL

(FROM AEBERSOLD VOL. 12)

RHYTHM CHANGES
(FROM AEBERSOLD VOL. 47)

102

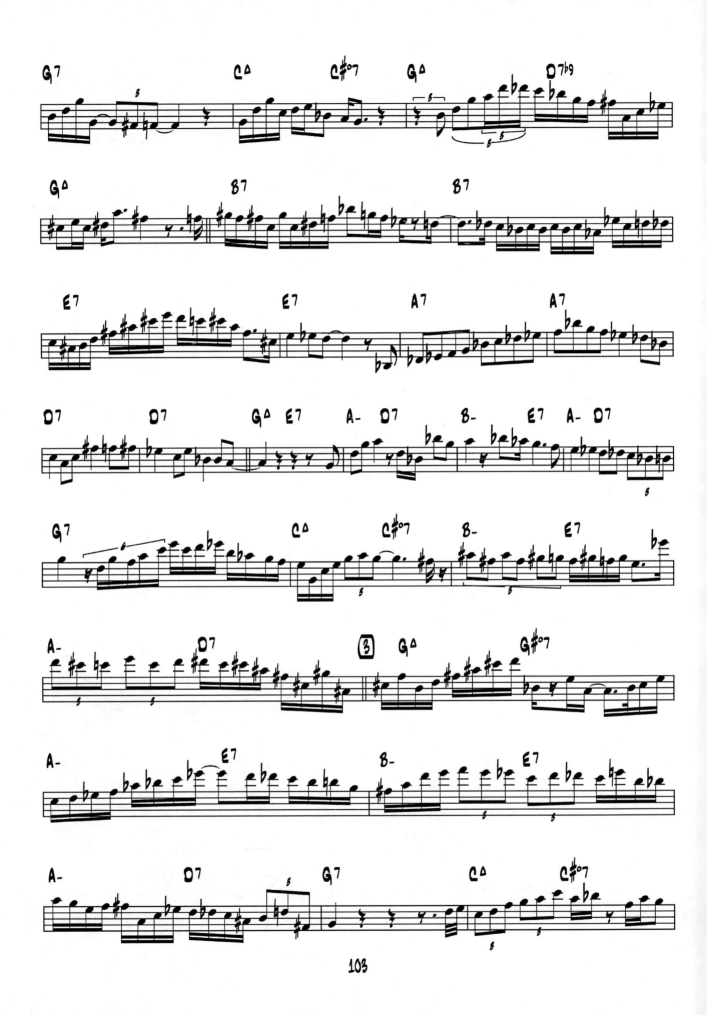

103

David Liebman's superimposed chord changes to:

IMPRESSIONS
(from Aebersold vol. 28)

(Each chorus played AABA)

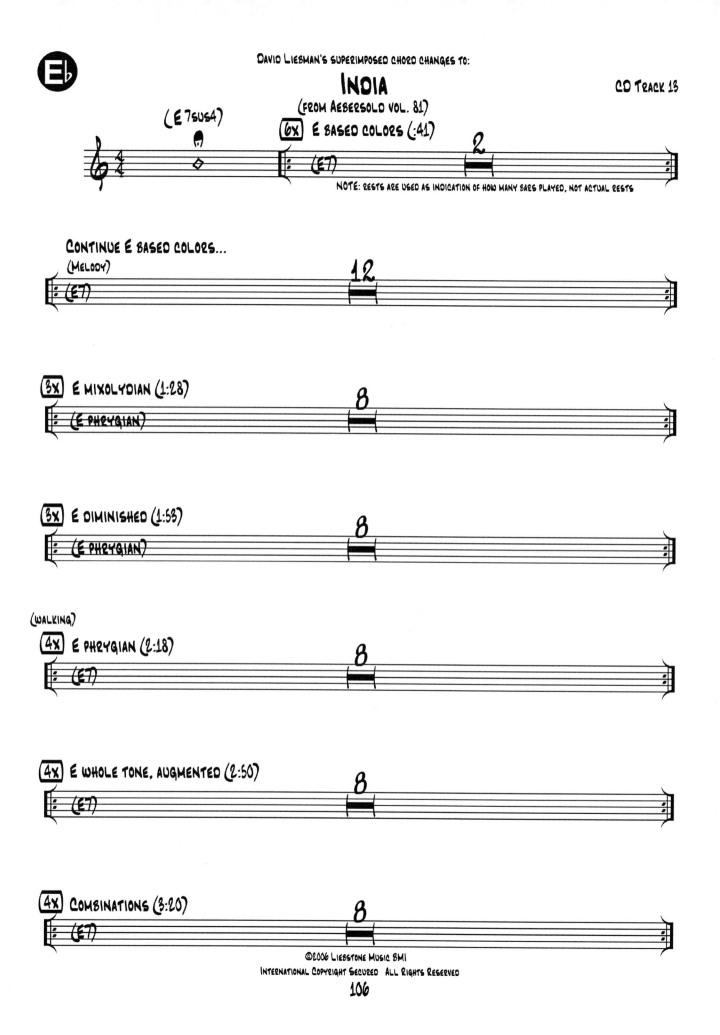

David Liebman's superimposed chord changes to:

LOFT DANCE

(from Aebersold vol. 19)

(PIANO INTRO) · 6 · (DRUM INTRO) · 8

LONG NOTES AROUND MELODY AND ORIGINAL PROGRESSION

(3X) | Eb△(#4) | G#△(#4) | G- | F7

NOTE: EACH CHORD IS PLAYED FOR 4 BARS THROUGHOUT!

SUPERIMPOSED— C△(#4) | F△(#4) | C- | G7

(3X) (1:00) | Eb△(#4) | G#△(#4) | G- | F7

F△(#4) | D△(#4) | A- | C7

(3X) (1:45) | Eb△(#4) | G#△(#4) | G- | F7

G7$^{\#9}_{\#5}$ | Eb- | E+ | D-

(2X) (2:29) | Eb△(#4) | G#△(#4) | G- | F7

A- | C7 | D7$^{\#9}_{\#5}$ | G△(#4)

(3X) (2:59) | Eb△(#4) | G#△(#4) | G- | F7

COMBINATIONS...

(3:43-END) | Eb△(#4) | G#△(#4) | G- | F7

David Liebman's solo on:
A Love Supreme
(from Aebersold vol. 28)

109

COMBINATIONS (3:15)

110

David Liebman's solo on:
Off A Bird
(from Aebersolo Vol. 81)

CD Track 16

Major and Minor 2nds, 3rds, 6ths (0:40)

Maj. and Min. 7ths and 9ths (1:55)

COMBINATIONS (2:15)

113

114

JAMEY AEBERSOLD JAZZ® PLAY-A-LONGS

Each Play-A-Long contains at least one stereo CD and a coordinated booklet with parts FOR ALL INSTRUMENTS. The volumes do not necessarily get progressively more difficult. Popularly termed *"The Most Widely-Used Improvisation Tools On The Market!"*

The special stereo separation technique is ideal for use by rhythm players.
The left channel includes bass and drums, while the right channel contains piano or guitar and drums.

"Anyone Can Improvise" by Jamey Aebersold
BEST-SELLING DVD ON JAZZ IMPROV!
2-HOUR DVD Featuring Jamey

JAMEY'S SUGGESTED ORDER OF STUDY: Volumes 1, 24, 21, 116, 2, 54, 3, 70, 5, 84, etc. **Vol. 1 and 24** work to form a strong foundation.

☑	VOL.#	TITLE	FORMAT	☑	VOL.#	TITLE	FORMAT
❏	1	"JAZZ: HOW TO PLAY AND IMPROVISE"	BK/2CDs	❏	67	"TUNE UP"	BK/CD
❏	2	"NOTHIN' BUT BLUES"	BK/CD	❏	68	"GIANT STEPS"	BK/CD
❏	3	"THE II/V7/I PROGRESSION"	BK/2CDs	❏	69	CHARLIE PARKER - "BIRD GOES LATIN"	BK/CD
❏	4	"MOVIN' ON"	BK/CD	❏	70	"KILLER JOE"	BK/CD
❏	5	"TIME TO PLAY MUSIC"	BK/CD	❏	71	"EAST OF THE SUN"	BK/CD
❏	6	CHARLIE PARKER - "ALL BIRD"	BK/2CDs	❏	72	"STREET OF DREAMS"	BK/CD
❏	7	MILES DAVIS	BK/CD	❏	73	OLIVER NELSON - "STOLEN MOMENTS"	BK/CD
❏	8	SONNY ROLLINS	BK/CD	❏	74	"LATIN JAZZ"	BK/CD
❏	9	WOODY SHAW	BK/CD	❏	75	"COUNTDOWN TO GIANT STEPS"	BK/2CDs
❏	10	DAVID BAKER - "EIGHT CLASSIC JAZZ ORIGINALS"	BK/CD	❏	76	DAVID BAKER - "HOW TO LEARN TUNES"	BK/CD
❏	11	HERBIE HANCOCK	BK/CD	❏	77	PAQUITO D'RIVERA	BK/CD
❏	12	DUKE ELLINGTON	BK/CD	❏	78	"JAZZ HOLIDAY CLASSICS"	BK/CD
❏	13	CANNONBALL ADDERLEY	BK/CD	❏	79	"AVALON"	BK/CD
❏	14	BENNY GOLSON - "EIGHT JAZZ CLASSICS"	BK/2CDs	❏	80	"INDIANA"	BK/CD
❏	15	"PAYIN' DUES"	BK/CD	❏	81	DAVID LIEBMAN - "STANDARDS & ORIGINALS"	BK/CD
❏	16	"TURNAROUNDS, CYCLES, & II/V7s"	BK/4CDs	❏	82	DEXTER GORDON	BK/CD
❏	17	HORACE SLIVER	BK/2CDs	❏	83	THE BRECKER BROTHERS	BK/CD
❏	18	HORACE SILVER	BK/2CDs	❏	84	DOMINANT 7TH WORKOUT	BK/2CDs
❏	19	DAVID LIEBMAN	BK/CD	❏	85	ANDY LAVERNE-"TUNES YOU THOUGHT YOU KNEW"	BK/CD
❏	20	JIMMY RANEY w/GUITAR	BK/CD	❏	86	HORACE SILVER - "SHOUTIN' OUT"	BK/CD
❏	21	"GETTIN' IT TOGETHER"	BK/2CDs	❏	87	BENNY CARTER - "WHEN LIGHTS ARE LOW"	BK/CD
❏	22	"FAVORITE STANDARDS"	BK/2CDs	❏	88	"MILLENNIUM BLUES"	BK/CD
❏	23	"ONE DOZEN STANDARDS"	BK/2CDs	❏	89	"DARN THAT DREAM"	BK/CD
❏	24	"MAJOR & MINOR"	BK/2CDs	❏	90	"ODD TIMES"	BK/CD
❏	25	"ALL-TIME STANDARDS"	BK/2CDs	❏	91	"PLAYER'S CHOICE"	BK/CD
❏	26	"THE SCALE SYLLABUS"	BK/2CDs	❏	92	LENNIE NIEHAUS	BK/CD
❏	27	JOHN COLTRANE	BK/CD	❏	93	"WHAT'S NEW?"	BK/CD
❏	28	JOHN COLTRANE	BK/CD	❏	94	"HOT HOUSE"	BK/CD
❏	29	"PLAY DUETS WITH JIMMY RANEY" w/GUITAR	BK/CD	❏	95	"500 MILES HIGH"	BK/CD
❏	30A	"RHYTHM SECTION WORKOUT" - PIANO & GUITAR	BK/CD	❏	96	DAVE SAMUELS - "LATIN QUARTER"	BK/CD
❏	30B	"RHYTHM SECTION WORKOUT" - BASS & DRUMS	BK/CD	❏	97	"STANDARDS WITH STRINGS"	BK/CD
❏	31	"JAZZ BOSSA NOVAS"	BK/CD	❏	98	ANTONIO CARLOS JOBIM w/GUITAR	BK/CD
❏	32	"BALLADS"	BK/CD	❏	99	TADD DAMERON - "SOULTRANE"	BK/CD
❏	33	WAYNE SHORTER	BK/2CDs	❏	100	"ST LOUIS BLUES" DIXIELAND	BK/CD
❏	34	"JAM SESSION"	BK/2CDs	❏	101	ANDY LAVERNE - "SECRET OF THE ANDES"	BK/CD
❏	35	CEDAR WALTON	BK/CD	❏	102	JERRY BERGONZI - "SOUND ADVICE"	BK/CD
❏	36	"BEBOP AND BEYOND"	BK/CD	❏	103	DAVID SANBORN	BK/CD
❏	37	SAMMY NESTICO	BK/CD	❏	104	KENNY WERNER - "FREE PLAY"	BK/CD
❏	38	"CLASSIC SONGS FROM THE BLUE NOTE JAZZ ERA"	BK/2CDs	❏	105	DAVE BRUBECK - "IN YOUR OWN SWEET WAY"	BK/CD
❏	39	"SWING, SWING, SWING"	BK/CD	❏	106	LEE MORGAN - "SIDEWINDER"	BK/CD
❏	40	"'ROUND MIDNIGHT"	BK/2CDs	❏	107	"IT HAD TO BE YOU!" - STANDARDS FOR SINGERS	BK/2CDs
❏	41	"BODY AND SOUL"	BK/2CDs	❏	108	JOE HENDERSON - "INNER URGE"	BK/CD
❏	42	"BLUES IN ALL KEYS"	BK/CD	❏	109	DAN HAERLE - "FUSION"	BK/CD
❏	43	"GROOVIN' HIGH"	BK/CD	❏	110	"WHEN I FALL IN LOVE" - ROMANTIC BALLADS	BK/CD
❏	44	"AUTUMN LEAVES"	BK/CD	❏	111	JJ JOHNSON	BK/CD
❏	45	BILL EVANS	BK/CD	❏	112	COLE PORTER - "21 GREAT STANDARDS"	BK/2CDs
❏	46	"OUT OF THIS WORLD"	BK/CD	❏	113	"EMBRACEABLE YOU" - BALLADS FOR ALL SINGERS	BK/2CDs
❏	47	"I GOT RHYTHM CHANGES" - IN ALL KEYS	BK/CD	❏	114	"GOOD TIME"	BK/4CDs
❏	48	DUKE ELLINGTON - "IN A MELLOW TONE"	BK/CD	❏	115	RON CARTER	BK/2CDs
❏	49	"SUGAR" w/ORGAN	BK/CD	❏	116	"MILES OF MODES" - MODAL JAZZ	BK/2CDs
❏	50	MILES DAVIS - "THE MAGIC OF MILES"	BK/CD	❏	117	"COLE PORTER FOR SINGERS"	BK/2CDs
❏	51	"NIGHT & DAY"	BK/CD	❏	118	JOEY DEFRANCESCO - "GROOVIN' JAZZ" w/ORGAN	BK/CD
❏	52	"STARDUST"	BK/CD	❏	119	BOBBY WATSON	BK/CD
❏	54	"MAIDEN VOYAGE"	BK/CD	❏	120	"FEELIN' GOOD" - BLUES IN B-3 w/ORGAN	BK/CD
❏	55	JEROME KERN - "YESTERDAYS"	BK/CD	❏	121	PHIL WOODS	BK/CD
❏	56	THELONIOUS MONK	BK/CD	❏	122	JIMMY HEATH	BK/CD
❏	57	"MINOR BLUES IN ALL KEYS"	BK/CD	❏	123	"NOW'S THE TIME" - JOEY DEFRANCESCO TRIO w/ORGAN	BK/CD
❏	58	"UNFORGETTABLE STANDARDS"	BK/CD	❏	124	"BRAZILIAN JAZZ"	BK/CD
❏	59	"INVITATION" w/ORGAN	BK/2CDs	❏	125	"CHRISTMAS CAROL CLASSICS"	BK/CD
❏	60	FREDDIE HUBBARD	BK/CD	❏	126	RANDY BRECKER w/RANDY BRECKER	BK/2CDs
❏	61	"BURNIN'"	BK/CD	❏	127	EDDIE HARRIS - "LISTEN HERE"	BK/CD
❏	62	WES MONTGOMERY	BK/CD	❏	128	DJANGO REINHARDT - "GYPSY JAZZ" w/GUITAR	BK/CD
❏	63	TOM HARRELL	BK/CD	❏	129	A JAZZY CHRISTMAS	BK/CD
❏	64	"SALSA, LATIN, JAZZ"	BK/CD	❏	130	"PENNIES FROM HEAVEN"	BK/2CDs
❏	65	"FOUR & MORE" w/ORGAN	BK/2CDs	❏	131	"CRY ME A RIVER"	BK/CD
❏	66	BILLY STRAYHORN - "LUSH LIFE"	BK/CD	❏	132	"ON THE STREET WHERE YOU LIVE"	BK/CD
		All prices subject to change without notice. Visit www.jazzbooks.com for current pricing information.		❏	133	"DOWN BY THE RIVERSIDE" - DIXIELAND CLASSICS	BK/CD